To Elisa and Grace, whose curiosity about the world inspired this entire series.

Laura

To Dad,

Thank you for introducing me to the worlds of Narnia and Perelandra when I was little. Thank you for encouraging me to dream, for telling me stories, and for drawing me closer to Jesus through them.

Keila

C.S. Lewis

Illustrated by Keila Elm | Design and Art Direction by André Parker
"The Good Book For Children" is an imprint of The Good Book Company Ltd
thegoodbook.com | thegoodbook.co.uk | thegoodbook.com.au | thegoodbook.co.nz
ISBN: 9781802543193 | JOB-008304 | Printed in India

Do Great Things for God

C.S. Lewis

The Boy Who Loved to Ask Big Questions

Laura Caputo-Wickham

Illustrated by Keila Elm

Jack was born in Belfast, into a home full of books.

There were books in the study, books in the drawing room, books in the bedrooms, and even books in the bathroom!

Jack spent many rainy days reading, and soon he started writing his own stories too. He wrote stories set in magical lands filled with talking animals.

Jack's name wasn't actually Jack. It was Clive Staples. But he didn't like that name and insisted that everyone call him Jack, after his favourite dog.

Today, many of us know him as C.S. Lewis.

Jack was a bright boy with a curious mind, and he asked lots of questions.

Some were small questions.

Some were BIG questions.

When Jack was nine years old, his mum became very ill and died. And an even bigger question filled his heart:

Sadly, bad things kept on happening. Jack's grandfather died too, followed by his uncle. Jack's dad became quiet and moody.

On a breezy September day, Jack boarded a ship to England, where he was going to study.

But his new boarding school was a miserable place, and he felt sad and very lonely.

And that's when Jack asked the biggest question of all: "Is God even real?"

A very big war spread across the world. It was known as the "Great War", though today we call it World War One.

Like many other young men, Jack bravely fought against the enemy – until an explosion hurt him badly and he had to be sent home.

It was 1918, and at 11 a.m. on the eleventh day of the eleventh month, the war ended. Jack could finally go back to the thing he loved most – books!

He studied at the University of Oxford and loved studying so much that he never stopped!

He became a teacher and made many friends.

One of these friends was J.R.R. Tolkien, who, at the time, was writing a book called *The Lord of the Rings*, the story of a group of brave hobbits going on an adventure.

Jack and Tolkien would talk for hours. Sometimes, they talked about God too. Tolkien believed in God and was happy to answer Jack's questions.

And Jack had lots of questions!

Jack began to read the Bible, where he learned more about Jesus, who loves us so much that he gave his life to pay for our sins so that we can have life for ever with God.

"The law of the LORD is perfect," says Jack's favourite Psalm, and it's thanks to this perfect book, the Bible, that we can find the answers to our questions.

And that's what happened to Jack. The more he read, the more it all made sense. And one day, while riding a motorcycle on the way to the zoo, he decided to follow Jesus as his Lord!

Now that he'd found the answers to his many questions, Jack wanted to help others find their answers too.

And he did that through stories.

Some were short stories, published every week in a newspaper. Some were longer stories.

But they were all very popular, and they helped people understand more about God.

When another war, called World War Two, began, people were feeling lost and scared.

"Would you talk about God on the radio?" a friend asked Jack.

And so, one Wednesday at 7:45 p.m., Jack explained the Bible to anyone who'd listen. He did the same the next Wednesday, and the Wednesday after that. More than a million people tuned in every week to find out how the Bible could answer their own questions.

One day, a picture of a faun carrying an umbrella popped into Jack's mind. Inspired, he wrote *The Lion, the Witch and the Wardrobe*, a story set in a magical land filled with talking animals, brave children and a fearless lion called Aslan, who gave his life for those he loved – just like someone else Jack had come to know very well.

And though life didn't get much easier, Jack knew he could always count on that same fearless love as described in the Bible, because, in that perfect book, Jack had found the answers to all his questions...

And Jack had lots of questions!

C.S. Lewis (known as Jack)

1898 – 1963

"The law of the Lord is perfect."

Psalm 19:7

Questions to Think About

1. Which part of Jack's story did you like best?

2. Jack loved asking big questions! Do you have any questions you would like to ask God? See if you can find the answers in the Bible. You may want to ask an adult or older Christian to help you.

3. One of Jack's questions was the biggest of all: "Is God even real?" Imagine a friend asking you the same question. How would you answer them? (Clue: Can you find the answer in the Bible? Or could you tell them something about Jesus? Or talk about a time when God has answered one of your prayers?)

4. What ideas does Jack's story give you about how you might serve Jesus when you are older?

5. What is one truth about God that you'd like to remember from this story?

C.S. Lewis

29 November 1898 Clive Staples Lewis was born in Belfast, in what is now known as Northern Ireland. He was the youngest of two children. When his beloved dog, Jacksie, died, Clive Staples adopted his name and wouldn't answer to anything else. Later, he allowed it to be shortened to Jack.

23 August 1908 Jack's mum, Flora, died of cancer. A month later, Jack joined his brother, Warren, at a boarding school in Watford, England. The school was not a happy place, and when it closed two years later, Jack returned to Belfast to study closer to home.

26 April 1917 Jack began his studies at the University of Oxford. As World War I progressed, he joined the British army, and on the day of his 19th birthday, he was sent to the front lines in France. When a British shell missed its target, Jack was wounded in the explosion and returned home.

1925 Jack began teaching at the University of Oxford. Soon after that, he bought a house called "The Kilns", where he lived with his brother as well as the mother and sister of Paddy Moore, a dear friend of his who had died in the war.

1931 After a long talk on Christianity with his friend J.R.R. Tolkien, Jack became a Christian. In *Surprised by Joy*, one of his books, Jack says, "When we [Jack and his brother] set out [by motorcycle to Whipsnade Zoo] I did not believe that Jesus Christ was the Son of God, and when we reached the zoo I did".

1941 Jack wrote *The Screwtape Letters*, a series of letters between a senior devil and a junior one, in which they discuss ways to tempt people to do bad things. The letters were published weekly in a newspaper and were later turned into a novel. Still not keen on his name, Jack wrote his novels with the name C.S. Lewis.

1942 During World War II, Jack gave a series of short radio talks about his faith. Later, these talks were published in his book called *Mere Christianity*.

1950 *The Lion, the Witch and the Wardrobe* was published. This was the first of seven books in the popular series called The Chronicles of Narnia.

1952 Jack met Joy Davidman, an American poet and writer. The two became very good friends and, a few years later, got married. Sadly, Joy became very unwell and died shortly after that.

1963 Three years after the death of his wife, Jack died too, leaving behind his powerful words, which, to this day, continue to help many people, young or old, to learn more about God and find answers to their questions.

World Map

Where in the world did Jack's story take place?

ASIA
AFRICA
AUSTRALIA

Interact with Jack's Story!

4-7s

All About

C.S. Lewis

Known as Jack

My Drawing of Jack

Where did Jack grow up?

What did Jack do on rainy days?

Why was he known as Jack?

What Did Jack Do When He...

Circle the Answer

What Did Jack Do When He...	Circle the Answer
Moved to England	Went to school to study **or** Went to work at a zoo
Became friends with J.R.R.	Opened an ice-cream shop with him **or** Talked to him about God
Was riding a motorcycle to the zoo	Decided to move to Belfast **or** Decided to follow Jesus as his Lord
Was asked to talk about God on the radio	Explained the Bible to listeners **or** Said no because he was too scared
Imagined a faun carrying an umbrella	Wrote The Lion, the Witch and the Wardrobe **or** Bought an umbrella

1

What Are 8 Things You Liked about Jack's Story?

5.

6.

7.

8.

Remember this Verse Jack Loved

"The law of the LORD is perfect."

Psalm 19 v 7

Can you say it all by yourself?

Family Activity: Come up with 5 animal characters and draw pictures of them. Try to write a short story together using your characters.

2

Download Free Resources at

thegoodbook.com/kids-resources

Do Great Things for God

Inspiring Biographies for Young Children

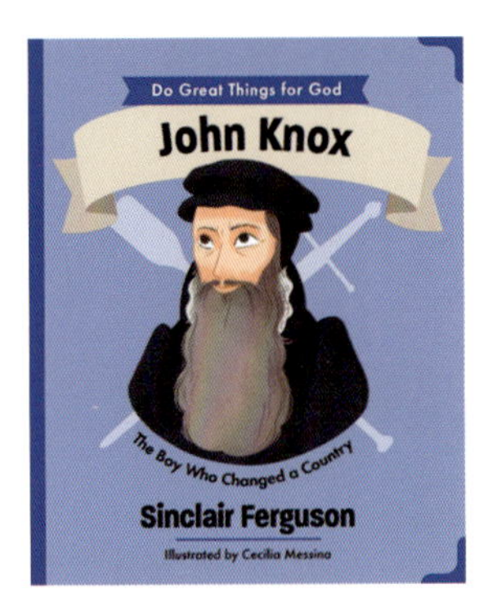

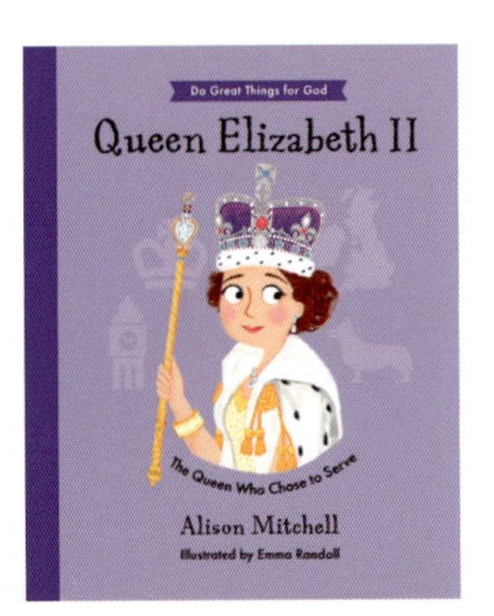

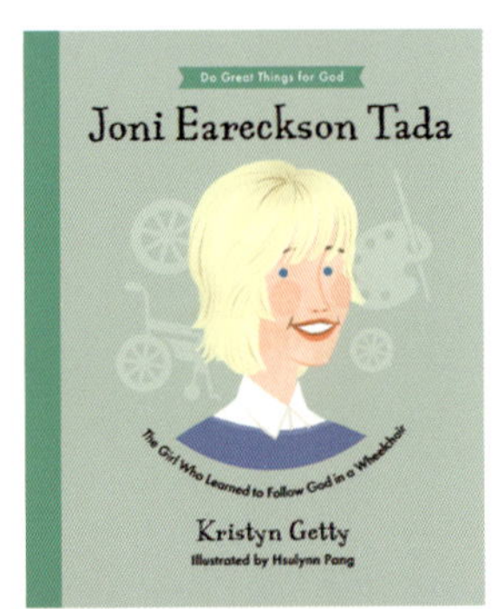

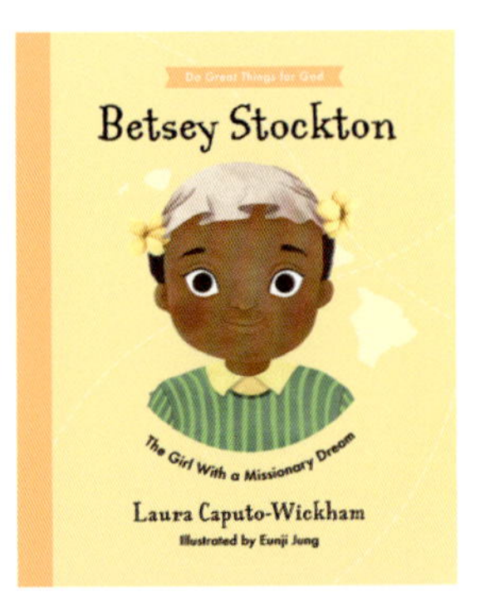

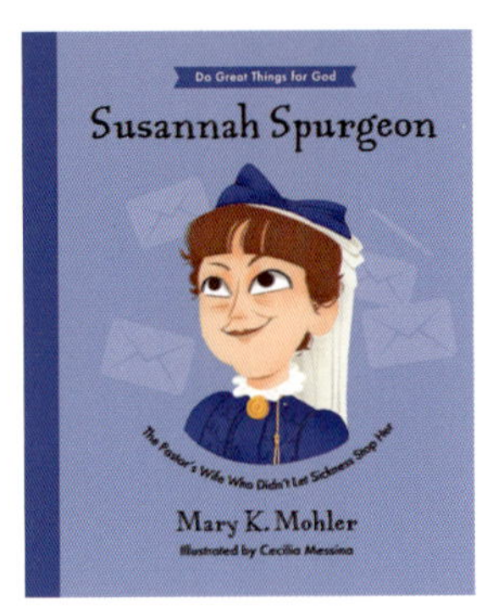

thegoodbook.com | thegoodbook.co.uk